Unpolished rice, the staple food of the Orient; - Primary Source Edition

Clubb, Henry Stephen, 1827- [from old catalog]

INDEX TO RECEIPTS

UNPOLISHED RICE,

—THE STAPLE FOOD OF THE ORIENT—

By Rev. Henry S. Clubb.

The endurance on long marches; the wonderful activity, bravery and success of the soldiers of Japan, and their comparative freedom from camp diseases* and rapid recovery from wounds resulting in so many victories over their flesh-fed enemies who have been defeated and routed in every important engagement, fully confirm the views advanced in the following address delivered two years ago before the Vegetarian Society of Philadelphia. The address was published in the *Rice Journal* at the time, and extracts have appeared in many periodicals. It is now presented in full, as the events of the war and the growing interest in the subject of health foods seem to call for a more extensive diffusion of the information contained therein:

My friends and members of the Vegetarian Society:

My attention was called to the subject of rice, by observing the great muscular development and strength of the athletes of Japan, who are said to train chiefly, if not entirely, on a diet of rice. A correspondent in Connecticut inquired if I could procure him a sample of Japanese rice, as he had understood it was richer in protein or flesh-forming element than the South Carolina rice commonly grown in this country.

Wheat here is considered so much richer in flesh-forming elements that rice in the Middle, Western and Northern States is used only as a dessert, in the form of puddings, or blanc mange, whereas in the Southern, or rice-producing, states, it is served daily as a vegetable, largely taking the place of white potatoes in the daily meals.

---

*General Oku's Headquarters, Feb. 1, 1905.—In nine months there have been but 40 deaths from disease in the immense army commanded by General Oku, a record that is believed to be unequaled in the world's warfare. * * * The percentages of the other Japanese armies are believed to be about the same.—Phila. Record, Feb. 2, 1905.

Our investigations have led us to believe that the more general use of rice as an article of daily food, not merely as an occasional dessert, would result in a diminution of dyspepsia and an increase of health, vigor, and vivacity throughout the continent of America.

The fact that the Japanese are the most artistic, humane, vivacious, and happy people on the face of the earth; and that their chief food is rice, is, on its face, a strong argument in favor of the more extensive use of that cereal.

Finding a good sample of Japanese rice in Philadelphia, I sent it to the Agricultural Department in Washington, inquiring if it had been analyzed, and received a very courteous reply from Mr. Ernst A. Bessey, Assistant in Charge of the Bureau of Plant Industry, United States Department of Agriculture, who wrote from Washington, April 19, 1902, that: "So far as I know, no comparative analysis has been made to determine whether Japanese rice contains more nitrogen than South Carolina rice. The fact is that the American method of milling rice so as to give it a high polish, as shown by the sample you enclose, loses about 90 per cent. of the nitrogenous matter in the grain, as this is contained in the fine polish which is taken off. In Asia, however, rice is not polished, so that the nitrogenous matter remains on the grain, and, as a result, the grain is much more nutritious."

The United States Agricultural Department kindly referred my letter to Prof. Knapp, of Lake Charles, La., who in due time sent the following valuable and interesting reply:

"Lake Charles, La., April 22, 1902.

"Rev. Henry S. Clubb, Philadelphia, Pa.

"Dear Sir:—At the request of the Department of Agriculture, I will undertake to answer your letter of April 7, 1902. I have not the analysis of the Japan rice before me, but my recollection is that it is richer in fats than other rices, but not in protein compounds, or flesh-formers.

"Being richer in fats, it has more flavor than other rices. The reason the Japanese are so muscular is that they do not polish their rice. In American mills the outside coating of the rice kernel is rubbed off. The process is as follows: 1st. The outer husk is removed. 2nd. The bran, just within the husk, is removed. 3rd. The solid kernel is then rubbed, to remove the rough protein surface and to give the kernel a gloss. This is called polishing, and the material removed is called polish, one of the most nutritious substances in all the cereals. Polishing removes more than three-fourths of the flavor and about one-fourth the fiber material. In Japan, China, and India polishing is not done, except for foreign markets.

"The Japanese army in the advance on Peking out-footed the armies of Russia, Germany, England, France and America. The Japanese soldier is fed on rice, with a ration of beans and fish. He can double-quick for fourteen hours, and repeat it for days.

"The Japanese or Chinese may be shot through the body, and if no vital part is cut, they scarcely notice the wound.

"If you will send to Dr. W. C. Stubbs, Audubon, New Orleans, La., I think you will get an analysis of Japan rice.

"Very truly yours,

"S. A. Knapp."

Agreeably to Prof. Knapp's suggestion, I wrote and received from Dr. Stubbs the following reply, dated "Audubon Park, New Orleans, La., May 1, 1902:

"There is no perceptible difference between analysis of Japanese rice and South Carolina rice. We make them indiscriminately and have made both quite a number of times. A few years ago, we undertook an examination of the by-products of the rice mill, and published the results in Bulletin No. 24. Unfortunately, this edition is exhausted, but I send you a later bulletin on rice, on page 400 of which you will find the analysis of the different products. By adding to the rice, the polish, analysis of which is given, and turning to page 399, you will see the amount of polish obtained there from 95 pounds of clean rice, and by putting the two together you can easily get the analysis of the rice after the bran is removed. If you desire the analysis of the rough rice with the bran and polish, you can simply take the rough rice, the amount of hulls with their analysis, and the remainder will be the rice with the polish and bran thereon.

"I should imagine that you could make arrangements with any of the rice mills in this city or state to complete the process of cleaning the rice at any point you desire it. At present it is not a merchantable article, but arrangements might be made with any of our mills to furnish you with the rice just simply hulled, as you desire. By writing to any one of the rice mills in this state, of which we have over fifty, you can doubtless make such arrangements.

"Very truly yours,

"WM. C. STUBBS."

These letters led to correspondence with rice millers and others engaged in the rice industry, and we received from the Agricultural Department, Washington, and from the Milling Companies in Louisiana, a mass of information on this subject, of which the following is a condensation:

In the rice districts of the United States rice is used as a vegetable, or in place of Irish potatoes. In other parts of the country rice is used chiefly boiled, flaked, rice puddings, croquettes, fritters, cakes, etc.

One hundred pounds of cleaned rice contains 87.7 pounds of nutrients, consisting of eight pounds protein—flesh-forming—3 fat, 79 carbohydrates, .4 ash. In comparison with this 100 pounds of wheat contains 87.2 pounds of nutrients, 10.8 of protein, 1.1 fat, 74 carbohydrates, .4 ash.

Rice is easily digestible. The tables of Profs. Atwater and Woods in Bulletin No. 7 of the Storrs Experiment Station, September, 1891, show that rice is fully as digestible as wheat flour, (fine) Maize meal, and more so than bread or potatoes. (Armory Austin B. S.)

It is claimed that rice digests in a healthy stomach in one hour, while two hours is the average time required for digestion of food.

Among cereals and grains, rice unquestionably stands first in importance in regard to the number of persons who consume it, the area devoted to its cultivation, and the amount annually produced thereof in the whole world. It has been stated that rice forms the principal, and, in some cases, the only food of from one-third to one-half of the whole human race. (Armory Austin B. S.)

The population of other rice-consuming countries in Asia and Africa may be roughly estimated at about 80,000,000 and the total of all the rice-consuming countries reaches 796,000,000 people, or 54.2 per cent. of the total population of the earth. (Armory Austin B. S.)

China and its dependencies have a population of 404,000,000, or 27.5 per cent. of the total population of the globe, and rice certainly forms the principal food supply of its people. The same may be said of India, with its population of 273,000,000, or 18.6 per cent. of the total population. In Japan, with a population of 39,000,000, rice forms 51 per cent. of the total sustenance. (Armory Austin, B. S.)

Even in America, Europe and Australia, where wheat, rye, maize, and other cereals are largely used, there is a large quantity of rice consumed.

Sir Wm. Berkeley, Governor of Virginia, caused half a bushel of rice (probably brought from England whither it had been received from India,) to be sown in her colony, and it produced sixteen bushels of good rice. This was in 1647. Rice was introduced to South Carolina in 1694. An English or Dutch ship was driven by stress to seek shelter in Charleston Harbor, and the captain visited Governor Smith, whom he had met in Madagascar. Smith expressed a desire to experiment with the growing of rice upon a low patch of ground in his garden; whereupon the captain presented him a small bag of rice seed which happened to be among his ship stores. The seed was brought from Madagascar, but may not have been grown there. It was planted in the garden in Longitude Lane, Charleston—the spot is still pointed out—and thus originated the important industry of rice cultivation, still flourishing in South Carolina.

There is a story that the Earl of Shaftsbury sent 100 pounds of the rice seed to Charleston about the same time, from the produce of which sixty tons of paddy were shipped to England in 1698.

Lowland rice was introduced to Louisiana in 1718, and upland rice into South Carolina, in 1772, from Cochin, China.

In this way the rice plant from its Asiatic home has made the circuit of the earth, and is now cultivated throughout the torrid zone and in the warmest parts of both temperate zones wherever there is abundant water supply.

Its geographical limits are said to be 45 degrees N. and 38 degrees S. latitude in the Eastern and 36 degrees N. to 38 south latitude in the Western Hemisphere. It is believed that it could be profitably grown in New Jersey, as well as all the states south of that state.

In China, Japan and Java soy sauce, soy bean cheese, or a similar product, is eaten with rice in considerable amounts, and furnishes a large part of the protein necessary for the daily diet of laborious people.

Dr. S. A. Knapp in Farmers' Bulletin No. 110 states that "Fashion demands rice having a fine polish, which removes some of the most nutritious portions of the rice grains. The Oriental custom, much used by farmers in the South, of removing the hulls and bran with a pounder and using the grain without polishing is economical and furnishes a rice of much higher food value than the rice of commerce. In the process of polishing nearly all the fats are removed. Upon the theory that the flavor is in the fats, it is easy to understand the lack of flavor in commercial rice and why travellers universally speak of the excellent quality of the rice they eat in Oriental countries."

The Engelberg Huller Company, of Syracuse, writes: "The people of the Northern part of the United States do not know the value of rice as a food. Two hundred times as much should be used as there is now."

The Star Rice Milling Company, of Crowley, La., wrote, May 8, 1902:

"We do not sell rice in the unpolished state for the simple reason that it is not salable. Rice is an article that is sold entirely on its appearance, although we are candid to say that the unpolished rice contains more nutriment. But the public demands polished rice, and we have to give it to them. You could probably make arrangements to buy unpolished rice if you desire it. Rice is the greatest food in the world."

Farmers' Bulletin No. 110, United States Department of Agriculture, speaking of the polish, or rice flour, says: "This polish is the germ and cuticle, and, like all other grains and fruit as it comes next to the skin is the sweetest part of the grain or fruit." The Engelberg Huller Company, commenting on the above, wrote, "I am satisfied that, if they would grind into flour what they save for the rice of commerce and analyze it, they would find it worth less than the polish. But that is not the style."

The Engelberg Huller Company, engaged in the manufacture of rice mills, wrote April 29, 1902, "You are correct in your surmise as to the polishing of rice. There is no question but what the high finish, or polish, given rice is at the expense of both quality and quantity. In rice-eating countries, where they use rice as a staple article of food, they do not ask for this high polish that people of the North especially, demand, as they want the dish to look nice."

I understand from the same company that the griddle cake flour known as "Aunt Jemima's" is made of one-third rice, one-third wheat, one-third corn and baking powder. All that is required is milk enough to make it the right consistency for muffins, etc. It is exceedingly good."

The Crowley Rice Milling Company, in kindly furnishing samples, wrote under date of Crowley, La., May 8, 1902: "If you could make this country a visit, you would get much valuable information that would assist you in your lecture and would be interesting to your audience. Crowley is the largest rice-shipping station in the United States, and it is claimed by a great many people that it is the largest in the world. We have now eight large rice mills in this city and two more in the course of construction with a possibility of a third."

The samples of rice furnished by the Crowley Milling Company, Crowley, La., were shown in clear glass jars and explained to the audience by which they were examined carefully, questions being asked and answered.

No. 1. Crowley's Best Head Rice. A very handsome sample of polished Japanese rice, having the appearance of pearls. This is now a very popular rice with the trade. It is grown in Louisiana from seed imported from Japan. It is considered richer in fat than other rice.

No. 2. Cream of the Rice Field. This contains 87.7 per cent. of nutrients of which 8 are protein, 79 carbohydrates, .3 fat, .4 ash. It is a large grain, long and plump.

No. 3. Japanese Head Rice. Very similar to No. 1.

No. 4. Unpolished Rice. This is the common South Carolina rice simply hulled and not polished. It is almost a pure white, and, when cooked, could scarcely be distinguished from the polished rice in appearance, and, being richer in fat and protein, is superior to the best Head Rice as a flesh former. (It was the intention of the lecturer to exhibit some of this in a cooked form, but, being accessible to the family provider, it had been used for cooking in preference to any of the other samples. The Vegetarian Society is obtaining a supply of this unpolished rice, and, when it arrives, will send samples by mail to all applicants as the object is to show that unpolished rice is so much better than the polished article.)

No. 5. Rice Polish. This is rice flour that has been rubbed off rice in polishing. It is richer than rice in flesh-forming elements, having 11.7 per cent. of protein, 7.3 per cent. of fat, 64.3 per cent. of carbohydrates. It is one and three-fourths times more valuable as food than polished rice. (Samples of this are being obtained by the Vegetarian Society to distribute to members and other applicants. It is a rich food, but its keeping character in hot weather is not yet established. It requires to be kept in a cool, dry place during the summer season.)

No. 6. Screenings. Simply the rice broken during the process of thrashing and hulling. It is as good as whole rice, although its being broken reduces its market value. It is screened from the head rice to improve its appearance.

No. 7. Brewers. This is a much smaller broken rice, apparently screened from the screenings to make them more salable, and is usually sold to brewers.

No. 8. Stone rice. This is rice partially hulled before being perfected in the hulling machine.

No. 9. Rough. This is rice simply thrashed and removed from the straw with the hulls on. It somewhat resembles barley before being pearled. It is commonly called "paddy."

No. 10. Rice Bran. This is a sample of the bran removed from the rice after it is hulled, but before it is polished. It has somewhat the appearance of what the wheat millers used to call "shorts" or "sharps," bolted from the fine flour to make it look whiter. It is richer in protein than any other product of the rice mill, containing 12.1 per cent. of protein, 8.8 per cent. of fat, and 59.4 per cent. of fibre and carbohydrates.

The lecturer also exhibited a small sample of Mexican rice, presented him by the Geo. L. Squier Manufacturing Company, at Buffalo, N. Y., who are large manufacturers of rice machinery and grain and nut mills. It is somewhat smaller than the head rice of South Carolina.

After these samples had all been discussed, small cups of rice coffee were served, made from rice browned in the oven.

AFTER THE LECTURE.

The Rev. Dr. MacPherson in expressing his great interest in the subject discussed, said the same principle had been of late years applied to the wheat flour industry, as it had been discovered that the best part of the wheat kernel was that nearest to the bran, and that had been, until recently, removed by the bolting process, in order to make a very white flour. The new machinery introduced was to preserve this important nitrogenous element in the flour, and, hence, "a whole wheat flour" now obtainable in all the stores.

As an incident, illustrating the swelling quality of rice while cooking, the lecturer referred to the dilemma a new cook on board a steamer found himself in, when, being ordered to serve boiled rice for the passengers, he filled a boiler with rice in the dry state, adding water. It soon overran the sides of the boiler. He scooped some out and put it into another boiler with water; but still it continued to swell and overrun, until every cooking vessel available was filled and yet it continued to overrun; and the amateur cook found himself at his wit's end to know what to do with the overflowing rice.

PREPARATION OF UNPOLISHED RICE.

The use of material to give lustre to the polished rice may have given rise to the directions given in cook-books and the practice of good cooks to "thoroughly wash," and even "rub with a cloth, and then rinse again the rice," but this is not necessary with unpolished rice as nothing is used to give it a pearly lustre and a single rinsing and picking out of any particles of dirt or of seeds will suffice.

It is desirable for a family supply to begin the day with a good stock of

1. PLAIN BOILED RICE.—If rice is to be used as a vegetable to be eaten with omelets or nut preparations, such as Protose, Nutose or Meatose, etc., it should be boiled so as to retain the distinctive character of the kernals. The method common in the Southern States,is to use a porcelain or granite-ware stewpan; put into it four cupfuls of water and let it come to a boil, adding a teaspoonful of salt. While still boiling, add gradually of the prepared rice, one cupful. With a fork, lift it once or twice, shaking the kettle so that none of the kernels stick to the bottom, and allowing the water to bubble through the grains. Let it boil twenty minutes; remove from the fire, pour off water, if any remains, and place on back of the stove or in the oven where it will finish swelling without burning. In this way the rice will be plump, light, and white. We believe with unpolished rice less salt is needed than with polished rice to produce the desired flavor, as the polishing process removes those elements which salt is required to replace. In fact, unpolished rice without salt is richer in flavor than polished rice is with salt.

2 RICE FOR MOULDING.—If rice is desired to form moulds or cups, solid to be served with jelly, jam or stewed fruit, as a dessert, it requires at least ten minutes more boiling. A farina or double kettle is desirable in this case, and when it is well boiled, it may be pressed into cups or moulds, previously dropped in water; a weight should be placed upon each while cooking, so as to make it solid and retain its shape when turned out. The moulded rice is a very convenient summer dish, as it can be served at any meal throughout the day and eaten with fruit; is exceedingly palatable and wholesome. It should be prepared in the morning and it will be ready for any unexpected visitors during the day. When the double boiler is used, milk may be substituted for water, if desired, but the genuine richness of unpolished rice can be best discerned when water only is used in cooking. The milk when used should come to a boil before adding the rice. A great variety of dishes can be prepared from the rice thus cooked, and it is desirable to have a good supply so as to be prepared for any emergency, as other dishes can be quickly prepared from it.

3. BAKED RICE.—Some persons cook rice, putting it into the oven in the evening and in the morning it is ready for breakfast. The heavy bean-pot with cover is suitable for this purpose.

4. STEAMED RICE.—Put one cup of rice into a porcelain ish with three cups of cold water, set in a steamer and cook three ours. Add boiling water if necessary, but do not break the grains.)ne cup of raisins or a cup of figs or dates, cut fine and care- .illy stirred in with a fork when the rice is half done, makes an greeable dessert pudding.

5. MOULDED RICE; English Method.—Eight ounces of rice, nd three half pints of milk. Swell the rice in the milk till all of ie milk is absorbed, and the rice thoroughly softened. Press it ito a mould with a weight upon it. Serve it turned out with pre- erved or stewed fruit.

6. CREAM OF ASPARAGUS AND RICE SOUP.—Cut two unches of asparagus into inch lengths and simmer them gently in 'ater until tender. Pour into a colander and press through all the nder parts of the asparagus. Into a soup kettle, put two table-)oonfuls of butter or olive oil, and stir into it four tablespoon- ıls of riceflour, brown, and gradually add the asparagus stock ıbout one quart), let boil two minutes; then add a pint of sweet ıilk or cream. Season to taste and serve with buttered toast ice.

7. CREAM OF CELERY WITH RICE.—Cream of celery ıay be made same as cream of asparagus, taking the outside alks and stumps of two bunches. It should be boiled for about ıe hour and then prepared same as asparagus and rice.

8. RICE AND ONION SOUP.—In one ounce of konut or ıtter fry till a light brown two or three large onions sliced ıin; add two tablespoonfuls of flour and brown till about the ıme color. Mix thoroughly with a pint of water; place over the re in a soup kettle, and when it comes to a boil, pour in a quart boiling milk, into which a cup of boiled rice has been mashed a smooth paste. Continue boiling till done; season to taste and rve.

9. POTATO AND RICE PUREE.—Lightly brown one inced onion in a saucepan with one teaspoonful of butter or onut. Add two minced potatoes and fry a little while. To this ld two quarts of water and allow to boil twenty minutes. Add ılf a cup of boiled rice. Pour the whole through a sieve and put ıe puree back into the soup kettle. When ready to serve, add

one cup of cream, with one tablespoonful of butter or konut and seasoning.

10. CREAM OF RICE AND SWEET POTATO.—Boil until tender, nine medium sized sweet potatoes and remove the skins. Sieve through a strainer the potatoes and one cup of boiled rice. Put the whole into a soup kettle with four tablespoonfuls of butter or konut and a little salt. Let boil a while and add two quarts of boiling milk. Stir well and serve with fried toast.

11. GRANOLA AND RICE SOUP.—Let two quarts of water boil, and when boiling add half pound of granola or re-baked bread crumbs, nicely ground. Let cook three quarters of an hour, stirring from time to time. Add half cup of boiled rice and let it boil a while longer. Add three spoonfuls of butter or konut, and one glass of milk. Do not let it boil after the milk is added.

12. RICE AND PEA SOUP; English.—Four ounces of split peas; four ounces of rice; one ounce and a half of butter (or oil), and salt to taste. Steep the rice and peas twelve hours in a half pint of soft water, to which a small piece of carbonate of soda, the size of a pea, has been added; pour off the water not absorbed. Digest these in a glazed covered jar in the oven, or boil slowly in a porcelain lined boiler from four to six hours; add chopped parsley with the butter, and seasoning thirty minnutes before the boiling is completed.

13. RICE SOUP.—Take boiled rice (2) and put it through a potato ricer and return to the double farina kettle with a cup of heated milk and seasoning. Into a cup of cream, beat well, three eggs. When the rice is stirred smooth in the milk, take from the fire and add the cream and beaten eggs. Add more seasoning if desired and serve with salted wafers.

14. CREAM OF RICE AND ALMOND SOUP.—Blanch one pound of almonds; drain; put all except twelve, into a mortar with one glass of milk, and one cup of boiled rice. Mash up finely and mix with one quart of milk. Let warm, but not boil. When ready to serve, blend with two spoonfuls of rice flour, one teaspoonful of sugar, one half teaspoonful of salt and two tablespoonfuls of butter mixed with one glass of cold milk. Split

the blanched almonds you have saved, put them in a tureen and pour the cream over.

15. RICE AS A VEGETABLE.—Pick and wash in warm water a pound of the best rice; set it on the fire with two quarts of boiling water and a small teaspoonful of salt; boil it till about three parts done (15 minutes), and drain it in a sieve immediately. Butter a pan; put in the rice; place the lid on tightly; set in a moderate oven till the rice is perfectly tender, and serve in a vegetable-dish. Prepared in this way, every grain will be separate and quite white.

16. STEWED RICE.—Put one half ounce of butter into a pot and fry in it until brown, an onion sliced; then add a half pint of hot water, half cup of rice, pepper, salt and cayenne. Cover and stew for fifteen or twenty minutes or until the rice is tender. Stir frequently to keep from burning. Serve.

17. RICE STEW WITH CHEESE.—Prepare as for stewed rice and when done add to it one ounce of grated cheese, stirring it thoroughly through the stew and serve, or the cheese may be sprinkled over the stew as it is served.

18. RICE CURRY.—One can of tomatoes, six tablespoonfuls of rice, one onion, salt, one saltspoonful of curry powder, white pepper and one tablespoonful of butter. Put the butter in a saucepan, grate into it the onion, add the liquor of the tomatoes, rice and seasoning (salt, pepper and curry powder). Simmer for about an hour on back of stove.

19. RICE EGG BALLS.—Boil hard five eggs; remove the shells and put through a potato ricer or a sieve with an equal amount of boiled rice (1.) Season with salt, pepper and butter. Make into balls and dip into raw egg; then in crumbs and fry in deep hot konut. Drain and place on small pieces of buttered toast, pouring over the whole, melted butter.

20. RICE OMELET.—Beat separately three eggs, add to yolks one-third cup of milk, one half cup of rice, two tablespoonfuls of butter, a little salt and pepper and lastly the whites. Cook over a gentle fire.

21. RICE, FRIED.—Rice boiled in milk and flavored with orange or lemon. To it add sugar and milk. When cold cut in

pieces, roll each piece in cracker crumbs; then in white of an egg; then in cracker crumbs and egg again. Fry in hot konut.

22. RICE TORTILLAS.—Make a dough of half pint of flour; half pint of ground rice, half cup of milk, a tablespoonful of butter, a little salt. Knead it thoroughly. Take pieces and put between the hands until it makes a large round, very thin cake. Bake on a griddle until brown.

23. RICE CROQUETTES.—To one cup of well boiled rice (2), add two yolks of eggs, a pinch of salt, a half cup of flour, in which one heaping teaspoonful of baking powder has been sifted. Mix well together and add enough milk to thin, and lastly fold in the well beaten whites of two eggs. When ready it should be of a consistency to drop from a spoon easily. Have ready a pot of hot konut; drop in by the spoonful and turn very soon. When brown and cooked through, take out onto brown paper or folded cheese-cloth and serve in a folded square of white linen.

24. SWEETENED RICE CROQUETTES.—To the above may be added a tablespoonful of sugar, making a sweetened croquette.

25. A SIMPLER RICE CROQUETTE.—Omit any of the ingredients in No. 23, which may not be at hand, using the boiled rice, seasoned to taste, rolled in bread crumbs and fried in konut.

26. RICE CUTLETS.—Fry two grated onions brown, add four tomatoes in the same pan and cook till tender. Cook a small cupful of rice in a double saucepan, turn it into a basin, add the onions and tomatoes, a teaspoonful of chopped parsley, half a teaspoonful of lemon thyme, two ounces of bread crumbs, one egg, and season to taste. Mix well, turn out on plates and smooth with a wet knife. Cut into fingers and fry crisp in egg and bread crumbs. Serve with tomato or egg sauce.

27. RICE AND TOASTED CHEESE.—Cut squares of cold, well boiled rice, (2) and fry in konut or oil until a rich brown. Cut cheese into squares about half as large, hold on a fork to the fire and when softened place quickly on a square of boiled rice. Serve immediately. The fried squares of rice are also good without the cheese.

28. ORANGE SNOWBALLS.—Boil two cupfuls of rice for fifteen minutes; drain and let cool; pare six nice oranges, being

careful to remove the white skin; spread the rice, in as many portions as there are oranges, on pudding cloths; place the orange in the center and tie; boil for one hour; turn out and sprinkle with sugar and serve with strawberry sauce.

29. RICE AU GRATIN.—Two cups of cold boiled rice, covered with a heavy cream sauce made with two teaspoonfuls of flour and butter, put in saucepan over the fire, one teaspoonful salt, one white pepper, teaspoonful onion juice, cup of milk. Pour over the rice and lightly stir. On top sprinkle bread crumbs, half-cup grated Parmesan cheese (American Creamery will do, but is not so good). Put this in a baking dish and bake five minutes.

30. OLIVE. RICE AND MUSHROOM SAUCE.—Prepare as for olive and rice sauce (32), putting in a quarter pound of canned mushrooms with their juice, one tablespoonful of rice flour and one tablespoonful of boiled rice. Let brown. Good to pour over savories.

31. TOMATO SAUCE.—Put butter or konut the size of an egg into saucepan; when it bubbles throw in a large onion chopped fine with two sprigs of parsley and a little pepper. Let it cook five minutes; then throw in a heaping teaspoonful of rice flour and a little hot water. Cook a few minutes; pour in a cup of strained tomatoes, stir well and pour over any savory omelet, or rice fritters.

32. OLIVE AND RICE SAUCE.—Stone twelve olives; mix with one tablespoonful of flour, one of boiled rice (2) with one and a half cupfuls of water. Boil five minutes.

33. MELANGE OF RICE.—Run through a food chopper enough vegetables to make one cup each of finely chopped cabbage, carrot, potatoes and turnips, add half cup of onion and half cup of celery. Put all into a kettle with two quarts of hot water and let boil one hour. Add salt, pepper and cayenne to taste. Let boil half an hour longer. Stir a cupful of milk into a cupful of plain boiled rice (1), warm, add a tablespoonful of butter or oil and mix all with the vegetables, but do not let the soup boil after adding the milk and rice.

34. RICE FRITTERS.—Six ounces of rice, and five eggs. Boil the rice, till quite soft, in as much water as it will absorb; put it in a basin, and when nearly cold, add the eggs well beaten, sea-

son, fry it in fritters of a light-brown color and serve with brown sauce.

35. GROUND RICE FRITTERS.—Quarter of a pound of coarsely ground rice, four eggs, a teaspoonful of parsley, and a teaspoonful of onions, both finely chopped.

36. RICE JELLY.—Mix a heaping teaspoonful of rice flour with enough cold water to make a smooth paste. Add a pint of boiling water, sweetened with two tablespoonfuls sugar and boil until clear. Flavor with lemon juice and mould.

37. RICE AND TAPIOCA PUDDING.—Soak one half cup of tapioca over night in a cup of water; in the morning drain off the water if any remains. Add to the tapioca half cup of rice, one cup of sugar, one cup of raisins, and eight cups of new milk, with a little grated lemon rind for flavoring. Put all in an earthen pudding dish on the top of the range where it will heat very gradually to the boiling point, stirring frequently. When the milk boils, put the pudding in the oven, and bake till the rice grains are perfectly tender, but not broken and mushy. From twenty minutes to half an hour is usually sufficient. When taken from the oven, it will appear quite thin, but after cooling will be of a delicious creamy consistency. Serve cold.

38. RICE FLOUR MOULD.—Braid two tablespoonfuls of rice flour with a little milk and stir the mixture into a pint of boiling milk, to which has been added three tablespoonfuls of sugar and a little salt, if desired. Let this boil until it thickens, then mould and serve with cream and sugar or with lemon, orange or other fruit sauce.

39. RICE AND STEWED APPLE DESSERT.—Steam or bake some rice in milk until tender, sweeten slightly and spread a layer of the rice half an inch thick on the bottom of a pudding dish, then a layer of lemon-flavored apple sauce, which has been rubbed through a colander and afterwards simmered on the range until stiff. If preferred, the sauce may be prepared by first baking the apples, and then rubbing the pulp through a colander. Add another layer of rice, then one of the sauce, and so on until the dish is full. Bake in a moderate oven and serve hot. If the apples are not very tart; part stewed and sifted cranberries may be used with them.

40. RICE SALAD.—One cup of cold rice, one chopped onion, some chopped celery. Mix all together, adding sufficient salad dressing to season. Serve on lettuce leaves.

41. RICE DRESSING.—One onion chopped fine, brown in one tablespoonful of butter, mix into this six cups of boiled rice and one cup of bread crumbs moistened in one cup of milk, add one cup of nut butter, one teaspoonful of salt, one-quarter teaspoonful of pepper, one-half spoonful thyme and a little chopped parsley.

42. RICE FLOUR CAKES.—One-half cup butter; one cup sugar; two eggs; one cup sweet milk, one and one-half cups rice flour; two teaspoonfuls baking powder; lemon flavoring. Bake in gem pans.

43. RICE PUDDING.—Six ounces of rice, one quart of milk, one ounce of butter, three ounces of sugar, four eggs, a little powdered cinnamon, and grated lemon-peel, or a few drops of almond flavor. Pick and wash the rice, set on the fire in cold water, and let boil about five minutes; then drain off the water and put the rice in a deep dish with the milk and a saltspoonful of salt; cover with a plate and set in a moderate oven; when the rice is sufficiently done, put in a basin and stir in the butter, sugar and seasoning; when nearly cold, add the eggs, well beaten; boil in a buttered basin, or bake in a pudding dish. Sultana raisins or currants may be added.

44. RICE BLANC-MANGE.—Three tablespoonfuls of rice flour mixed with a little cold milk, and one pint of milk. Stir well together and add three-fourths of a cup of sugar, the grated rind of a lemon and one-half teaspoonful of vanilla. Place on the fire and boil till it thickens (stirring constantly), then pour into moulds and allow it to cool. Turn on a dish and serve with whipped cream or stewed fruit.

45. RICE MERINGUE.—Steam a cupful of rice; first soak in one and a fourth cups of water for an hour, then add a cup of milk, turn into an earthen dish suitable for serving it from a table, and place in a steam-cooker or a covered steamer over a kettle of boiling water, and steam for an hour. It should be stirred with a fork occasionally, for the first ten or fifteen minutes. Heap loosely on a glass dish and dot with squares of cranberry or currant jelly. Beat the whites of two eggs to a stiff froth

with one-third cup of sugar and pile it roughly over the rice. Serve with cream.

46. BOILED RICE AND APPLE PUDDING.—Wash a cupful of good rice and steam until half done. Have pared and cored without dividing, six large, easy-cooking tart apples. Put a clean square of cheese cloth over a plate, place the apples on it, and fill them and all the interstices between with rice. Put the remainder of the rice over and around the apples; tie up the cloth and cook in a kettle of boiling water until the apples are tender. when done, lift from the water and drain well, untie the cloth, invert the pudding upon a plate and remove the cloth. Serve hot with cream and sugar or cocoanut sauce.

47. RICE FRUIT DESSERT.—Cold boiled rice, moulded so that it can be sliced, may be utilized in making a variety of delicious desserts. A nice pudding may be prepared by filling a dish with alternate layers of half-inch slices of moulded rice and grated tart raw apples the same thickness. Grate a little lemon rind over each layer. Cover, and place in the oven in a pan of boiling water, and bake for an hour. Serve with sugar and cream. Stoned cherries or peaches may be used instead of apples.

48. RICE PUDDING.—Three ounces of rice, a pint and a half of milk, two ounces of butter, three or four ounces of sugar, three eggs, and half an ounce of almonds, bitter and sweet mixed. Wash the rice and put into a dish with the milk and a very small portion of salt; set in the oven and let it remain till tender; turn into a basin and stir in the butter and about two ounces of powdered sugar, and when cold, add the yolks of the eggs, well beaten; melt a little butter in a dish and pour in the rice; then beat the whites of the eggs, adding the remainder of the sugar and the almonds, pounded; pour them on the top of the rice and bake about an hour in a moderately hot oven.

49. BOILED RICE PUDDING, WITHOUT MILK OR EGGS.—Six ounces of rice, and two ounces of currants. Wash and pick the rice; put into a saucepan with a pint and a half of cold water, adding a little salt; let boil gently, till all the water is absorbed; then add the currants or raisins, carefully washed and picked. Butter a pint basin, put in the rice, cover with a cloth, and let boil one hour.

50. GROUND RICE PUDDING.—Four ounces of ground rice, one quart of milk, two ounces of butter, quarter of a pound of sugar, five eggs, and a little almond flavor. Mix the rice with a little cold milk till smooth; set the remainder of the milk with a little cinnamon in it, over the fire and when boiling, add the rice gradually, and continue stirring till it has boiled a few minutes; then pour into a basin and stir in the butter and sugar well beaten and the almond flavor; bake either with paste round the dish or without, sift white sugar on the top and serve with currant jelly.

51. BOILED GROUND RICE PUDDING.—Six ounces of ground rice, one quart of milk, five eggs, quarter of a pound of sugar and one teaspoonful of salt. Set a pint and a half of new milk on the fire and when nearly boiling, add the rice, mix till quite smooth with quarter of a pint of cold milk; stir constantly till it thickens: pour into a dish and stir in the sugar and salt; when nearly cold, add the eggs, well beaten; boil an hour and a half in a buttered dish and serve with sweet sauce.

52. RICE CHEESECAKES.—Quarter of a pound of ground rice, one pint of milk, five ounces of white sugar, quarter of a pound of butter, and four eggs. Boil the rice in the milk, adding a piece of cinnamon: pour into a basin and when nearly cold add the butter melted, the eggs, well beaten; the sugar, powdered, and a few drops of almond flavor. Bake in small tins, lined with pie paste.

53. BAKED BANANAS AND RICE.—Place in a double kettle two cups of new milk and a teaspoonful of butter and a half teaspoonful salt and let it come to a boil. Now, add gradually stirring, a half cup of well warmed rice: cover closely, boil half an hour. Lay six ripe large bananas into pie-pan, pour over them hot water until the bottom of the pan is well covered and place them in a good steady oven, and bake until soft. Take from the oven, pour off water, if any, set back and dry off five minutes. Put a spoonful of the warm boiled rice on a plate, spread out a little and place on the top the baked bananas from which the skin has just been removed, bend it into a neat circle on the rice, drop a bit of good butter into the center and carry to the table hot.

54. FRUIT AND RICE.—Instead of bananas in the fore

going recipe any kind of fresh or canned fruit may be stubstituted, such as peaches, pears, plums, apricots, apples, fresh figs and all kinds of berries. The fruit may be used either fresh or stewed and if fresh the addition of sugar and cream helps very much some kinds.

55. BANANA FRITTERS.—Take one cup of rice flour and one-half cup of wheat flour, one coffee cup milk, one egg, half a teaspoonful salt, one and one-half teaspoonful of baking powder. Beat together the flour, half the milk and the yolk of the egg, salt and baking powder. Beat rapidly and well, whipping over and over (not merely stirring), and lastly fold in the beaten whites. Take up a spoonful, insert into it six slices of banana, cut across, close the incision, drop into hot konut and fry to a delicate brown, five or ten minutes.

56. RICE SNOWBALLS.—One cup of rice boiled and cooled. Whites of three eggs. Three spoonfuls of sugar and one teaspoonful of melted butter. Mix thoroughly and form into balls. Set on to a flat low dish, place in the oven and bake without browning, about ten minutes. Pour over this whites of three eggs beaten dry, to which three teaspoonfuls of pulverized sugar and half a teaspoonful of lemon extract are added. Set in a cool oven to just dry and not brown and serve with whipped cream.

57. RICE ALMOND FLAVORED SNOWBALLS.—Boil six ounces of rice in one quart of milk with sugar and a flavoring of almond until the rice is tender, adding a little more milk, should it dry away too much. When the rice is soft put it into teacups and let it remain till cool, then turn it out into a deep dish, pour over it a pint of custard and on the top of each ball place a bright colored piece of jelly. The custard should be made with the whites of eggs and seasoned with almond.

58. FRUIT RICE BALLS.—Into a double kettle put a pint of fresh milk and let it come to a boil, when it boils stir into it half a cup of rice, half a teaspoonful of salt, cover and let it boil fifteen minutes. Seed a half cup of raisins, wash and dry a half cup of currants, cut in thin slices citron, enough to make a half cup, beat one egg with the yolk of one more, with one-fourth of a cup of sugar. At the end of the fifteen minutes add the fruit to the rice and cook ten minutes longer. Just before taking from the

fire, add the beaten eggs, let stand five minutes and turn upon a flat dish. Press out to about two inches thickness, cut into cakes with a biscuit cutter, roll in beaten eggs, then in bread crumbs, and fry in hot konut. Serve with cream or any sauce.

59. RICE DUMPLING.—Steam a teacup of rice until tender, and line an oiled earthen pudding dish, pressing it up around the sides and over the bottom. Fill the crust thus made with rather tart apples cut in small slices; cover with rice, and steam until the apples are tender, which may be determined by running a broom-straw through them. Let stand until cold, then turn from the dish and serve with sugar and cream. Any easy-cooking tart fruit as stoned cherries, gooseberries, etc., may be used in place of the apples, when preferred.

60. RICE CREAM PUDDING.—Take one cup of good well washed rice, one scant cup of sugar and eight cups of new milk, with a little grated lemon rind flavoring. Put all into an earthen pudding dish and place on the top of the range. Heat very slowly until the milk is boiling, stirring frequently, so that the rice shall not adhere to the bottom of the dish. Then put into a moderately hot oven, and bake without stirring, till the rice is perfectly tender, which can be ascertained by dipping a spoon in one side and taking out a few grains. It should be, when cold, of a rich creamy consistency, with each grain of rice whole. Serve cold. It is best if made the day before it is needed. If preferred, the milk may be first flavored with cocoanut, according to the directions.

61. RICE PUDDING WITH RAISINS.—Wash thoroughly one half cup of rice, and soak for two hours in warm water. Drain off the water, add two tablespoonfuls of sugar, one half cup of raisins, and four cups of milk. Put in an earthen pudding dish and cook for two hours in a moderate oven, stirring once or twice before the rice begins to swell, than add a cup of hot milk and cook for an hour longer.

62. RED RICE MOULD.—Take one and one-half pints of red currants and one-half pint of red raspberries. The juice may be diluted with one part water or two of juice if desired. Sweeten to taste, and for each pint when boiling stir in two tablespoonfuls of ground rice or rice flour rubbed smooth in a little of the juice which may be retained for the purpose. Pour into moulds, cool, and serve with whipped cream.

63. RICE AND FRUIT DESSERT.—Steam a cup of good well-washed rice in milk till tender. Prepare some tart apples by paring dividing midway between the stem and blow ends and removing the core. Fill the cavities with quince of pineapple jelly; put the apples in a shallow stewpan with a half cup of water, cover and steam till nearly tender. Put the rice, which should be very moist, around the bottom and sides of a pudding dish; place the apples inside cover and bake ten minutes. Serve with cream flavored with quince or lemon.

64. RICE CUSTARDS.—One ounce and a half of ground rice, three ounces of loaf sugar and one pint of new milk. Boil the rice in the milk, adding the sugar, and a piece of cinnamon; pour it into custard-cups, in which a little fresh butter has been melted, and bake in a slow oven.

65. MOULDED RICE.—Eight ounces of rice, one saltspoonful of salt, and three pints and a quarter of milk. Wash the rice, pour the milk upon it, and boil slowly, in a brown basin, covered, in the oven, till it becomes tender, and the milk absorbed, pour into a mould and cover with a plate; turn out, either warm or cold and serve with preserves and cream.

66. PLAIN MOULDED RICE.—Eight ounces of rice, one saltspoonful of salt, and three pints and a quarter of water. Wash the rice; pour the water upon it and boil slowly in a brown basin, covered, in the oven, till it becomes tender and the water absorbed; dip a mould in cold water; pour in the rice and cover with a plate; turn out, either warm or cold and serve with preserved or stewed fruit.

67. MOULDED GROUND RICE.—Five ounces of ground rice, one quart of milk, four ounces of loaf sugar, half a saltspoonful of salt, and six drops of almond flavor. Steep the rice in a little cold milk while the rest of the milk is boiling; then add it to the boiling milk, with sugar; boil twenty minutes, stirring all the time; add the flavor; pour into a mould, previously dipped in cold water; let stand till cold and serve with preserves and cream.

68. PLAIN MOULDED GROUND RICE.—Six ounces of ground rice, two ounces of loaf sugar, six drops of lemon flavor or three drops of almond flavor and one quart of water. Steep the rice in a little of the water while the rest of the water is boiling; then

add it to the boiling water with the sugar; boil twenty minutes, stirring it all the time; add the flavor; dip the mould into cold water; pour in the rice, and let it stand till cold, serving with stewed or preserved fruit.

69. BREAD WITH A MIXTURE OF RICE.—Six pounds of flour, one pound of rice, one ounce and a half of German yeast, and one ounce of salt. Boil the rice in two quarts of water till soft; drain the water from it; mash, and mix the rice with the flour, adding the salt, and the yeast prepared as usual; mix with the water in which the rice was boiled, adding as much lukewarm water as required, and when risen bake the bread in the usual way.

70. RICE CORN BREAD.—Separate three eggs; to the yolks add a pint of milk and a tablespoonful of melted butter, a cupful of boiled rice, two cupfuls of corn meal and a half cup of flour. Beat thoroughly; add two teaspoonfuls of baking powder and fold in the well beaten whites. Bake in a shallow pan in a quick oven.

71. RICE CAKE.—Half pound of ground rice, ten ounces of sugar, six eggs and two ounces of bitter almonds. Blanch, and beat the almonds in a mortar and put them to the ground rice, adding the sugar, finely powdered, and the eggs well beaten and strained; beat all together about three quarters of an hour. Bake in a buttered mould, in a moderately hot oven.

72. RICE CAKE.—Half a pound of ground rice (not rice flour), half pound of white sugar, four eggs and a few drops of almond flavor. Beat the eggs a little and mix them with the rice and sugar; beat with a wooden spoon half an hour, adding the almond flavor; pour into a tin mould, warmed and well rubbed over with fresh butter, only filling it, and bake in a moderately hot oven. If baked in one, it will require about an hour; if in two, about three quarters of an hour.

73. RICE CAKE.—Half a pound of fine rice flour, quarter of a pound of the best moist sugar, one teaspoonful of baking powder, two eggs, half a pint of milk, three ounces of butter and one ounce of candied citron or lemon. Mix the baking powder well with the flour; add the citron, cut in small pieces, and the sugar; when mixed, add the eggs, well beaten, nearly half a pint of milk, and the butter, melted; mix all together; pour into two tin moulds, warmed and buttered which should only be about half filled and bake in a moderately hot oven.

74. RICE BISCUITS.—One pound of rice flour, one pound of loaf sugar, eight eggs, and a teaspoonful of essence of lemon. Mix the rice flour with the sugar, powdered; add the eggs, well beaten; the essence of lemon or a few drops of almond flavor and bake in cheesecake-tins made hot and a little clarified butter put in each, in a moderately hot oven.

75. RICE MUFFINS.—Dilute one cup of boiled rice with one cup of milk, one teaspoonful of melted butter, yolks of two eggs, one and a half cups of flour, one tablespoonful of sugar, half teaspoonful of salt, one heaping teaspoonful of baking powder. Fold the beaten whites of the eggs in carefully; pour into hot gem pans and bake in a quick oven.

76. RICE FLOUR MUFFINS.—One and one-half cups of rice flour, two cups of whole wheat Graham flour, a little salt, one and one-half tablespoonfuls of baking powder; sift these thoroughly together and add one pint of sweet milk and a little butter, and one well beaten egg. Bake in a hot oven twenty minutes.

77. RICE ROLLS.—Into one pint of scalded milk stir one pint of ground rice, two tablespoonfuls of sugar and one teaspoonful of salt. Beat thoroughly and add three well beaten eggs and bake in a hot oven twenty minutes.

78. RICE WAFERS.—Put one cup of boiled rice through a sieve and mix with it one cup of sifted flour, white of an egg, saltspoonful of salt, one tablespoonful of konut or butter, and enough sweet milk to make a biscuit dough. Put on moulding board and beat with rolling-pin for twenty minutes. Take a small piece of the dough roll between the hands and then roll out with rolling-pin as thin as possible, flour and place in tins and bake to a light brown.

79. GROUND RICE MUFFINS.—Take one quart of ground rice, add to it one ounce of butter, one teaspoonful of sugar and a little salt. Pour on enough boiling water to moisten all the meal, stirring all the time. Cool and add yolks of three well beaten eggs, then enough sweet milk to form a batter, beating thoroughly; add one tablespoonful of baking powder, moisten with a little water and lastly, fold in the whites of the eggs well beaten. Bake in muffin or gem pans in a quick oven.

80. TOMATOES STUFFED WITH RICE.—Take large smooth tomatoes, cut out of the stem end a piece as large as a dollar. With a spoon scoop out the inside, not too deep and fill this cavity with the following: One-half cup rice, well boiled, a tablespoonful of onions, fried in a teaspoonful of butter, and a little parsley. Bind these with a well beaten egg; season.

81. RICE GEMS.—A pint of buttermilk or sour milk, one egg, a teaspoonful of soda (or more if the milk is quite sour), a little sugar if desired, half teaspoonful of salt. Mix one-third whole wheat flour, (Graham), with two-thirds rice flour and beat into the milk and egg enough to make it the consistency of Graham gems. Drop into the heated gem pans and bake about fifteen minutes.

82. RICE GRIDDLE CAKES.—Boil a cup of rice; when cold mix thoroughly with one pint sweet milk, the yolks of four eggs and flour sufficient to make a stiff batter. Add one tablespoonful of melted butter. Stir in one teaspoonful of soda and two of cream of tartar and a little salt, fold in the beaten whites of the eggs and fry on a griddle. A nice way to serve is to butter them, cover with preserves or jelly, roll them up, sprinkle and serve hot.

83. RICE MILK.—Quarter of a pound of rice, and three pints of milk. Wash and pick the rice, and soak one hour in cold water; then pour off the water and set the rice on the fire with the milk and a little cinnamon, stirring it frequently; when sufficiently boiled, mix a dessertspoonful of flour with a little water and stir it well in, adding sugar and salt.

84. RICE ICE CREAM.—Put two heaping teaspoonfuls of rice flour into a double boiler, add slowly one quart of milk and two cups of sugar; cook for fifteen minutes, then add the beaten yolks of six eggs, cook for a moment and add the beaten whites of the eggs just before taking from the fire; when cold add one quart of cream and two teaspoonfuls of vanilla, then freeze.

85. RICE WATER.—Wash and pick two ounces of rice; set on the fire in a quart of water; boil gently till the rice is quite soft and pulpy; rub through a hair sieve, and sweeten with honey or sugar. Lemon juice may be added. Two apples sliced and boiled with the rice water, makes a pleasant summer drink.

86. RICE FLOUR WATER.—Mix one tablespoonful of rice flour with enough cold water to make a smooth paste, add two pints boiling water. Sweeten and boil till clear. Cool on ice and serve quite cold, but not iced.

87. RICE FLOUR BREAD.—One pint of fine rice flour in a warm bowl. Pour on it three pints of boiling water, stirring well. Cover and let it stand awhile to soften thoroughly. When cool add a little more yeast than for wheaten bread. Salt and shortening (konut), same as for wheaten bread. Work it thoroughly and set it to rise. When light, use wheaten flour enough to mould it into loaves. Put into pans; let rise and bake.

88. RICE FLOUR ROLLS.—Take the sponge of the Rice Bread (87), using as little wheaten flour as possible for moulding into rolls. Let rise till quite light and bake.

89. RICE FLOUR BATTER CAKES.—Make a batter with rice flour and very little wheat flour, using eggs or baking powder and bake on griddle.

90. RICE JOHNNY CAKE.—One egg beaten very light; one cup of milk; two cups of rice flour; one heaping teaspoonful baking powder; one teaspoonful sugar, and one of konut; salt to taste. Bake in oiled bread pan or muffin rings.

91. RICE WAFFLES.—To two cups of boiling water add a little salt and one cup of rice flour. Stir well and set aside to cool. When milk warm stir in one teaspoonful of soda and enough sour milk alternately with one-half cup of wheat flour to make a waffle batter. Lastly add a teaspoonful of melted butter or konut and two well beaten eggs.

92. ENTIRE RICE FLOUR MUFFINS.—Pour two cups of boiling water over a heaping teaspoon of butter or konut; while still boiling add a cup of rice flour and stir briskly. Remove from the fire and cover. When lukewarm add one teaspoonful of soda, half a cup of sour milk, and two eggs, beating well. Bake in greased muffin rings in a hot oven.

93. RICE POLISH BREAD.—Two cups of buttermilk or sour milk. Into this stir one and one-half teaspoonfuls of soda and a saltspoonful of salt. Then add two cupfuls of sifted rice polish and a large teaspoonful of melted butter. Beat two minutes and pour into a

buttered tin can or pail having a tight cover. Set into boiling water and boil continuously for two hours. Always replenish the kettle with boiling water. This comes out a rich brown loaf.

94. RICE POLISH STEAMED BREAD.—Into two cups of buttermilk or sour milk stir one and one-half teaspoonful of soda with a heaping saltspoonful of salt and a tablespoonful of sugar. Then add two cupfuls of sifted rice polish, a teaspoonful of melted butter, using more if sour milk is used, and a cup of washed and dried currants or any other fruit, cherries being preferred. Thoroughly mix and pour into a well buttered can or pail which has a tight cover. Set in boiling water and boil continuously for two hours. Add boiling water to the batter as needed. Serve with Fairy Butter.

95. FAIRY BUTTER.—Cream very thoroughly one teaspoonful of butter with one-half cup of sugar and season with lemon.

96. RICE POLISH GEMS.—Separate one egg, put the yolk into a bowl, beat until light, add one cupful of sweet milk and a saltspoonful of salt. Sift one cup of rice polish, stir into it one and one-half teaspoonfuls of baking powder and stir into the mixture. Fold the beaten whites in lightly and drop into heated gem pans. Bake fifteen minutes.

97. BUTTERMILK RICE POLISH GEMS.—Separate an egg and beat the yolk until light. Then add one cup of buttermilk or one cup of sour milk (if sour milk is used, add more butter). Stir into the milk a teaspoonful of soda and half a teaspoonful of salt. Beat and add one cupful of sifted rice polish. Beat until thoroughly incorporated, then fold in the beaten whites of the eggs. Bake in heated gem pans fifteen minutes.

98. SWEET RICE POLISH GEMS.—Same as 96, only add sugar to make a sweetened gem.

99. RICE POLISH PUDDING.—One cup of sifted polish, half or cup of flour, a heaping teaspoonful of baking powder, a tablespoonful of sugar. Sieve all these together so as to thoroughly mix them. Add one teaspoonful of butter or konut and mix all together with sweet milk and a well beaten egg. Use sufficient milk or water to make a rather stiff batter; then mix in half a cup of cleaned currants, seeded raisins or other dried fruit; flavor with nutmeg or other spice and pour into a well-buttered pudding bowl; place on

cover and steam for two hours. Serve with cream sauce.

100. RICE POLISH GRIDDLE CAKES.—A cup and a half of sifted rice polish, one cup of wheat flour, a teaspoonful and a half of baking powder. Beat up two eggs, adding a pint of milk and a saltspoonful of salt, a tablespoonful of melted butter or konut; lastly add gradually the polish, flour and baking powder, well mixed together. Stir to a batter and pour into cakes on a hot griddle.

101. NUTMEATO NO. 1.—As a savory, to eat with rice as a vegetable, the following preparation will be good. Two and a half cups of any good strong cereal coffee, two cups of nut butter, one cup of corn starch and one teaspoonful of salt. Mix the corn starch, butter and salt first, then put in the coffee by adding a little at a time and mixing until smooth. Put into a can or dish with tight-fitting cover, and cook in a closed steamer from three to five hours. Sealed cans give better results and may be used if desired. The sunken lid self-sealing cans are convenient for the purpose. The contents will be firm and can be turned out whole by cutting off the bottom of can with can opener, and when cool may be cut into slices and served with boiled rice.

102. NUTMEATO NO. 2.—One cup of nut butter, one cup of strained stewed tomatoes, half a cup of water, half a cup of corn starch or browned flour and salt to taste. Proceed as with No. 1.

103. RICE WITH NUTMEATO.—Cook rice in salted water, having it the consistency desired. Cut nutmeato (101) into cubes and distribute it evenly through the rice. Cook slowly without stirring again.

104. RICE FLOUR AS A MEDICINE.—Rice flour browned, makes a good food for babies with bowel trouble. Rice flour browned and mixed with olive oil makes a healing salve. Rice flour should be sprinkled over a wound that has proud flesh in it.

THE RICE CURE.—The fact that rice can be digested, ordinarily, in one hour should commend it to all persons with weak digestion and to such as do not take vigorous exercise.

Food has a controlling influence on the temperament of nations. The restless energy that beef-eating nations possess may become a disease. A diet largely of rice will tend to restore those equable conditions which belong to a well balanced system. The quiet patience of the Chinese and Japanese is due to rice. Irritable and nervous people should eat rice. The prevalent dyspepsia of Americans can be cured by making rice the staple food.

ANALYSIS OF RICE POLISH.—Rice Polish is the delicate outer coating of the rice kernel, which is removed in the form of flour, under the polishing process. It contains on an average: Water 10.0, ash 6.7, protein 11.7, fibre 6.3, nitrogen free extract 58.0, fat 7.3. This shows that it is rich in material for repairing the tissues of the body and for imparting heat and energy. It possesses high flavor and is easily digested. It is superlative food for the human family. Observe carefully the recipes and there will be added to the breakfast and dinner menu some most delicious and nutritive food.

Rice polish as an article of general consumption in Northern States is in its experimental stage. Its keeping qualities have to be established, but its highly nutritive value is unquestioned and makes it worthy of extensive experiment. It will, we believe, become a valuable addition to the economic food resources of America.

DR. J. H. KELLOGG.—In March, 1905, members of the Vegetarian Society met Dr. J. H. Kellogg at the sanitarium, Wallace Street, Philadelphia. Among other subjects discussed was that of unpolished rice, when Dr. Kellogg said that unpolished rice was 25 per cent. richer and more life-sustaining than the polished rice of the stores and he wanted to obtain it by the car load for making into puffed rice.

ACKNOWLEDGMENT.

For numerous suggestions, recipes, etc., which have enabled us to complete this little booklet, we are under obligations to the Penny Vegetarian Cookery (1849), Vegetarian Cookery by a Lady, 1849 (English), and to Science in the Kitchen (Mrs. Kellogg's), Guide to Nut Cookery (Mrs. Lambert's), the Rice Cook Book of the Southern Pacific R.R. Co., The Rice Journal and Southern Farmer (Mrs. Prof. Knapp), and Therapeutic Dietetics (Hazeldine), American.

JAPANESE METHOD OF COOKING RICE.—Quantity of water varies according to the qualities of rice, but five parts of water to four of rice or six parts to five, by volume, will be common proportion. 1st. Boil the water and then pour the rice, previously washed, into this boiling water, at the same time increasing the flame in furnace. The pan-cover must fit the pan edge as tightly as possible and also must be a heavy one, enough to withstand the high steam pressure in the pan, and if it is not heavy enough, put some weight on it. Keep the fire strong. In three or four minutes the steam pushes out of the pan; but let the fire be strong for three or four minutes more, and then, as quickly as possible, withdraw the blazing fire (in case of wood fuel) or make the fire very mild (in the case of oil or gas kiln) and let the pan stand on little under fire or very mild flame for twenty or thirty minutes. Then remove the pan from the furnace and let it stand for ten minutes more. This is all the process.

I hope you may try it. I think you can reach the right point after a few trials. Rice thus cooked is very delicious to the taste, and may be eaten by itself without any milk or sugar.

Very respectfully yours,

S. OTSUKA,

Director of Imperial Kiusiu Agricultural Experiment Station.

THE JAPANESE ARMY RATION.—The army ration in Japan is said to be 36 ounces of rice. When cooked, this quantity would weigh eight to ten pounds, an almost incredible amount of food for one day.

UNPOLISHED RICE might be adopted as the chief food on American tables with great advantage in health and economy.

BAKING POWDER.—Some of the recipes contain "Baking Powder" as one of the ingredients to be used. A correspondent objects that all baking powder contains alum. We are assured the Royal Baking Powder is an exception in this respect, and that it does not contain any injurious properties, its true formula being printed on each label.

We understand the Battle Creek Sanitarium Co. have a baking powder also that is unobjectionable.

It is understood that each cook will modify recipes according to what is desirable and available.

TESTIMONIALS.

FROM SARAH TYSON RORER,

April 18, 1905.

Dear Mr. Clubb: I am very glad to know that I can always purchase the unpolished rice from you. In my own family I never use the polished rice. It seems a pity to rob our most important and easily digested vegetable food of so much of its nourishment, for a slight difference in color. Unpolished rice contains sufficient nitrogen to form quite a perfect food—that is, it requires less nitrogenous material to make it well balanced, and such light food as eggs and milk easily digested, may be added in preference to heavy foods, as peas and beans. Rice, the most easily digested and important of all vegetable foods, is, when polished, as we usually find it in the markets, robbed of a large amount of its nourishment.

Yours truly,

SARAH TYSON RORER.

3307 Mt. Pleasant Street, N. W., Washington, D. C.

FROM MR. CHENWITH, DETROIT.

The unpolished rice which we are now using is very fine.

J. S. CHENWITH,

450 Pennsylvania Avenue, Detroit, Mich.

FROM DR. E. G. SMITH, DWIGHT, MASS.

Thanks for your letter and the unpolished rice. It is fine.

ELLEN GOODELL SMITH, Dwight, Mass.

FROM OTTO CARQUE, CHICAGO.

The rice sold in the United States to-day is unfit to eat and it will be a great boon to vegetarians if we can introduce natural rice which is equal if not superior in many respects to rye and wheat.

OTTO CARQUE,

Pres. of Cosmos Pub. Co., 765 N. Clark St., Chicago.

FROM SHAKER COMMUNITY.

Will you please send us one hundred pounds of unpolished rice?

DANIEL OFFORD,
Mt. Lebanon, N. Y., May 6, 1905.

FROM MISS ELEANOR M. JONES.

The peanuts were extra fine, and I am delighted with the (unpolished) rice.

MISS ELEANOR M. JONES,
Quogue, L. I., N. Y., May 15, 1905.

FROM DR. NORTON F. W. HAZELDINE.

St. Louis, Mo., April 13, 1905.

I have carefully read your lecture on "Unpolished Rice," and it is needless to say I endorse every word of it.

I have found it a very difficult thing to obtain unpolished rice in this country, so confine myself to Chinese rice exclusively. It is a very small grain, rich in oil and of a most pleasant flavor. Indeed I prefer it to any rice and eat it twice every day.

There is no doubt in my mind that rice is far more the ideal food than wheat, and where bread stuffs can injure the digestive activities, I have never found that rice did. Also barley, which forms the chief staple of the Arab, comes next to rice as a perfect food stuff, it never producing digestive disturbances.

I shall be most pleased to receive your new book and feel sure it will be of great interest and benefit to the work. With my kindest regards and best wishes, I am most cordially yours,

NORTON F. W. HAZELDINE.
Instructor in Physiological Culture and Dietetics, Studio 605
Mermod Jaccard Building.

Letters of similar purport are frequently received from persons prominent in the food reform movement.

VEGETARIAN SOCIETY SPECIALTIES

RECENT PUBLICATIONS.

The following booklets sent by mail from the office of the Vegetarian Society of America, 1023 Foulkrod St., Frankford, Philadelphia. Trade 50 per cent. discount.

THIRTY-NINE REASONS WHY I AM A VEGETARIAN. This is the result of a life-long experience, and contains a condensed outline of the Vegetarian System, with vignette of the author. By Rev. Henry S. Clubb. Ten one cent stamps.

A SUMMARY OF ARGUMENTS FOR VEGETARIANISM, by Rev. Wm. Penn Alcott. By mail five one cent stamps.

A MAY FESTIVAL OF THE PHILADELPHIA VEGETARIAN SOCIETY, with vignette of Anita Trueman. Two one cent stamps.

VEGETARIANISM FROM A BIBLE STANDPOINT, by Rev. Ellery Robinson. Five one cent stamps.

THE AMERICAN VEGETARIAN COOKERY. Two hundred and fifty recipes, compiled by the Ladies of the Bible Christian Church. Fifteen one cent stamps.

THE MESSAGE, every two months in the interest of the Bible Christian Church of Philadelphia, 25 cents a year; 5 cents a number.

THE SECOND INTERNATIONAL VEGETARIAN CONGRESS, held at the La. Purchase Exposition, September, 1904 with account of Health Food Commission. Ten one cent stamps.

UNPOLISHED RICE THE STAPLE FOOD OF THE ORIENT, on which the Japanese Army won its great victories and performed its rapid marches,. A lecture by Rev. Henry S. Clubb, to which are added directions for cooking it, over one hundred recipes, testimonials, etc. Fifteen one cent stamps. With sample of Unpolished Rice, by mail, 25 cents.

POLISH, five cents a pound. [illegible] mail, 6 cents. See analysis in [illegible] entitled, "Unpolished Rice, the [illegible] of the Orient."

WHOLE WHEAT GRAHAM FLOUR.

This is made from the best and cleanest wheat procurable, and is milled so as to reduce the size of the bran, making it digestible and harmless to the mucus membrane. Made into bread or pastry, it is a sure cure and preventative of constipation and its attendant evils. In 1-pound packages 6 cents. In bulk 5 cents a pound.

VEGETARIAN SOCIETY SOAP.

There are two kinds of soap used by those who discard the use of animal fat, viz.: one made of kerosene and cocoanut fat, and the other a castile soap made of olive oil. Both are excellent toilet soaps, and the first is used for removing spots from clothes with great ease and little rubbing. Some prefer it for laundry purposes, especially for fine 50 cents.
a pound. Olive Oil Castile, bar of 4 pounds,
linen. Sold at 5 cents a cake, 15 cents

UNPOLISHED RICE.

As unpolished rice contains 25 per cent. more fat and muscle-forming nourishment than polished rice, and has no paraffine on its surface, as much of the polished rice has, the Vegetarian Society has obtained a supply and will sell it as follows: Best head rice, 8c. lb.; Samples by mail on receipt of 10 cents, with lecture, 25 cents.

PURE ITALIAN OLIVE OIL

in sealed cans as imported from Italy, 60 cts. a quart, $2.50 a gallon, when ordered of the

VEGETARIAN SOCIETY,

1023 Foulkrod St., Frankford, Philadelphia

HYGIENIC KAUGHPHY.

This is Dr. Lovell's superior substitute for coffee. It has nearly the flavor, but without the stimulating effects of the coffee berry. Sold in 20-cent packages.

THE VEGETARIAN SOCIETY

will deliver a dollar's worth or more of any of its specialties, free of charge, to be called for at any of the railroad stations in Philadelphia and vicinity, where the railroads deliver packages to their patrons. Send cash for amount of goods desired, and state the station at which you will call for them.

VEGETARIAN SOCIETY,

1023 Foulkrod St., Philadelphia.

The Vegetarian

THIS MILL has been se[l]
best mill for domestic use.
ing nuts for nut meal or for nut
to perfection

WHOLE WHEAT GRAHAM FLOUR

UNPOLISHED RICE FLOUR

GRANOLA
and other Health Foods

The price is now reduced from $4.00 to $3.20; with improved hopper $3.85, on receipt of which the mill will be sent either from Philadelphia or from Chicago, as desired, when ordered from the VEGETARIAN SOCIETY OF AMERICA, Frankford, Philad'a.

PURE NUT BUTTER.

Every one who tastes the Nut Butter, made under direc- of the Vegetarian Society, by B. R. H. Clubb, will pronounce it the best nut butter obtainable. It is made of the highest grade Spanish peanuts, which are carefully hand-picked and made free from imperfect nuts or any foreign substance. Sold in glass jars at 15 cents, or air-tight cans at 30 cents each. four cans for $1.00.

1023 Foulkrod Street, Philadelphia

Sold by Up-to-date (

CPSIA information can be obtained at www.ICGtesting.com
Printed in the USA
LVOW09s1433250216
476693LV00016BA/253/P